CLASSIC WARPLANES

BAe/McDD
HARRIER

Mike Spick

SMITHMARK

A SALAMANDER BOOK

©Salamander Books Ltd. 1991
129-137 York Way,
London N7 9LG,
United Kingdom.

ISBN 0-8317-1409-3

This edition published in 1991 by
SMITHMARK Publishers, Inc., 112
Madison Avenue, New York, NY 10016.

SMITHMARK Books are available for
bulk purchase for sales promotion and
premium use. For details write or
telephone the Manager of Special Sales,
SMITHMARK Publishers, Inc., 112
Madison Avenue, New York, NY 10016.
(212) 532-6660.

All correspondence concerning the
content of this volume should be
addressed to Salamander Books Ltd.

This book may not be sold outside the
United States of America or Canada.

CREDITS

Editor: Chris Westhorp
Designer: Tony Jones
Color Artwork: ©Salamander Books Ltd.
Three-view, side-view and cutaway
drawings: ©Pilot Press, England
Filmset by: The Old Mill, England
Color separation by Graham Curtis
Repro, England
Printed in Belgium by Proost International
Book Production, Turnhout

AUTHOR

MIKE SPICK is a full time writer on military aviation subjects with a
particular emphasis on tactics. Consultant Editor to Air Forces Monthly,
he also lectures, makes occasional television appearances, and does consultancy work
for a European aerospace company. To date he has written more than 25 books,
including ''Fighter Pilot Tactics'' (Patrick Stephens) and ''The Ace Factor'' (Airlife)
while his many works for Salamander include ''Modern Air Combat'' and ''Modern
Fighting Helicopters'', both with Bill Gunston; ''F-14 Tomcat'', ''F/A-18 Hornet'',
and ''B-1B'' in the Fact File series; plus ''Fighter Combat'' and ''Attack Aircraft''
in the Illustrated Guides, as well as contributing to ''The Battle of Britain''.

CONTENTS

TODAY, the British Aerospace (BAe) Harrier is a familiar sight at air displays, demonstrating its short take-off, hover, and vertical landing capabilities, not forgetting the almost obligatory bow to the crowd as a finale. Its unique operational qualities tend to be taken for granted these days, and it is easy to overlook how near it was to becoming one of the legion of great British aircraft failures of the 1950s and '60s. Its Short Take-Off, Vertical Landing (STOVL) capabilities are now widely accepted as the inevitable result of demands for dispersed basing and the ability to operate from damaged airfields. But it was not always so . . . !

The original requirement for vertical or ultra short take-off for fixed-wing aircraft arose primarily from the need to intercept bombers, and was

Below: The Bachem Ba 349 Natter, designed in 1944 for vertical launch and parachute landing in sections.

first attempted by Germany during the Second World War. The German situation was at that time unique. While their conventional fighters were good by any standards, they were so totally outnumbered by Allied fighters that penetrating the escort screen for a successful attack on the bomber fleets was becoming daily more difficult. Technology appeared to provide the answer, with jet and rocket motors promising speeds that would make interception by the escort fighters highly improbable. Rocket motors also gave the sort of thrust-to-weight ratio which would permit vertical take-off, in addition to an unsurpassed rate-of-climb. Short on endurance, they would, however, permit the fighters to wait on the ground until the bombers approached. Vertical take-off held other advantages, in that no fuel would be wasted in taxying out and trundling down the runway to reach flying speed, thus maximizing endurance. Dispersed basing, and freedom from the need for conventional runways, was

not regarded as essential, although obviously, with Luftwaffe airfields being heavily bombed at frequent intervals, it was an added bonus.

A competition held in 1944 produced the Bachem Ba 349 Natter (Adder), a semi-expendable interceptor powered by four solid-fuel rockets for the vertical launch, and a throttleable liquid-fuel sustainer motor for the operational part of the flight. Designed for cheap and easy production by semi-skilled labour, the Natter carried 24 unguided rockets mounted in its nose. After the attack the pilot dived away, and once clear of enemy fighters he reduced speed. A series of actions then dismantled the aircraft; the pilot returning to *terra firma* under one parachute, doubtless just itching to do it again, while the rear section, containing the main rocket motor descended under another. If this was the competition winner, what must the losers have been like! The first piloted launch took place in February 1945; the pilot did not survive. It was really a surface-to-air missile equipped with a human guidance system. Not surprisingly, the Natter never entered service.

Another German project of the time was the Focke-Wulf Treibflugel. This was propelled by three ramjets located on the tips of three rotating wings; small rockets being used to accelerate it up to the ramjet operating speed of about 231mph (371km/h). It had four tail fins, each with wheels, upon which it squatted for take-off. Armament consisted of four conventional cannon. It was never built.

With the ending of the war, the German vertical take-off requirement collapsed, while the victorious Allies seemingly had no need for it. Then, with the commencement of the so-called Cold War, attitudes started to change. Clearly it was only a question of time before the Soviet Union possessed a formidable nuclear capability. In the foreseeable future, the means of delivery would be the fast, high-flying jet bomber. Before much longer, it also became evident that North Atlantic Treaty Organization (NATO) air bases in Central Europe were only a few minutes flying time away from the East German border, and were vulnerable to surprise attack.

VTOL

The defensive problem became twofold: firstly, how to reach the fast, high-flying raider in the short time available; and secondly, how to get off the ground with a minimum of delay in the event of a surprise attack. Some nations, Great Britain among them, dallied with the idea of a Natter-like rocket-powered interceptor which could be blasted off the ground at a steep or even vertical angle, to counter the fast and high bomber. With all fuel expended, this was to glide home (or to the nearest available flat surface) to land, and be recovered by a special vehicle. However, the logistics of recovery were horrendous and this idea was still-born.

The quick reaction requirement was experimentally met by Zero Length Launch (ZELL), which consisted of blasting a conventional fighter off a ramp with booster rockets, later to recover to a runway in orthodox fashion. Not least of the dangers to the pilot in this last system was the possibility of falling 30ft (9.15m) from the access ladder while attempting to enter the cockpit. ZELL was to prove unsatisfactory for many reasons.

Apart from the need to counter the high-flying bomber and the surprise attack, it also soon became evident

Above: The Rolls-Royce ''Flying Bedstead'' used two vertical lift Nene engines, with bleed air ducts on outriggers for control.

that airfields were vulnerable. The 1950s were the greatest years in aviation, and anything was worth a try. Vertical Take-Off and Landing (VTOL) seemed a valid method of freeing tactical fighters from the constraints of airfields, and many schemes were put in hand to develop it.

For effective vertical take-off, a thrust-to-weight ratio of about 1.2:1 is required. Older readers may remember that conventional fighters with such ratios exceeding unity first became fashionable in the 1970s, and prior to the 1950s this was only achievable by rocket propulsion. But in the years following, great advances were made in conventional powerplants, and the challenge then became to design an airframe light enough to

carry a worthwhile load of fuel and weaponry that could be propelled vertically upwards. The thrust also had to act directly through the aircraft's centre of gravity if assymetric loads were not to make it uncontrollable. This inevitably meant that the early VTOL jets were tail-sitters, which simplified matters in that a tail-sitter is a conventional aircraft with a very high thrust-to-weight ratio stood up on end.

The other problem was one of aerodynamic control at very low or zero speeds. Unless air is passing fairly rapidly over the control surfaces of an aeroplane, they do not work, as they have nothing to ''bite'' on. Some sort of reaction jet was needed, using either bleed air from the engine, or hydrogen peroxide thrusters. Either way, it had to be tied into the orthodox control system to avoid the pilot having two lots of controls to contend with. This would take a great deal of development

History and Development

effort, and was largely responsible for the profusion of "Flying Bedstead" test rigs that appeared in Great Britain, France, the United States and the Soviet Union at about this time. The Natter had been launched at high Gs under autopilot control, and so had not needed this refinement.

The first jet VTOL aircraft to fly was the Ryan X-13 Vertijet. This diminutive machine was almost literally built around a Rolls-Royce Avon 200 series engine, which combined the highest thrust with the lowest weight and also the smallest cross-sectional area. With little fuel and even less weapons-carrying capability, there was no way in which the Vertijet could have been developed into an operational fighter; it was simply a proof-of-concept aircraft. On 28 November 1956 it made the first ever transition from wingborne flight to the hover, and on 12 April 1957 it demonstrated a full cycle: taking off vertically and flying "around the block" before coming in for a vertical landing. But development of the Vertijet was terminated shortly after.

Several factors militated against the possibility of the Vertijet being turned into military hardware. Firstly, it was a tail-sitter. This put the pilot in an unnatural position for take-off and landing, and made extraordinary demands on his judgement, rather like reversing a very large car into a very small space, but with a dire penalty for failure. In part this was offset by a swivelling seat, but whether the average squadron pilot could have handled the bird is open to doubt. Secondly, it used what was laughably know as a trapeze for take-off and landing. This was a huge mobile hydraulic ramp, which raised the Vertijet from horizontal to vertical for take-off, and on which the Vertijet hooked itself for landing. It had been suggested that squadrons in the field could suspend themselves on wires

Above: The VJ-101C combined two lift jets in the fuselage with a pair of swivelling jets on each wingtip for lift and propulsion.

strung between trees or towers but this is scarcely believable. Just entering and exiting the cockpit would have been an operation fraught with immense difficulty; while servicing, refuelling and rearming, all difficult operations with a tail-sitter perched on the ground, would have been nearly impossible. These considerations made it inevitable that if VTOL was to succeed, the aircraft would have to be a flat-riser: a conventional machine capable of ascending and descending vertically.

THRUST VECTORING

There were two main avenues of approach for powering a flat-riser: thrust vectoring, and dedicated lift engines. Of these, the second solution was in many ways the simplest, consisting of a cluster of lift engines around the aircraft's centre of gravity, to be used only for take-off and landing; while providing an optimized engine or two

for conventional flight modes. The lift engines could be very simple, and therefore light, being required to run for only two or three minutes on each mission.

The main difficulty arises from the need to guard against engine failure in the hover; thrust assymetric to the centre of gravity is potentially lethal. One could cynically say that with many engines there is much more to go wrong. As dedicated lift engines mean extra weight to be carried, including structure, the associated plumbing, and the inlet and efflux doors, aerodynamically the aircraft will perform like a heavier version of its conventional self.

The French Dassault Mirage IIIV, which first flew on 12 February, 1965, was the only VTOL aircraft to attain Mach 2, which it did on 12 September 1966. No other VTOL or STOVL aircraft extant can achieve a speed anywhere near this. But weight apart, the carriage of lift engines (the Mirage IIIV had no less than eight) demands a big airframe, while the engines occupy volume better used for other things, such as fuel. The Mirage IIIV also needed a special pad for take-off and landing, and was not capable of performing a short rolling take-off, something that was essential to allow a worthwhile warload to be carried. It was also very costly: three Mirage IIIEs could be purchased for the same price. The programme was quietly allowed to lapse.

Thrust vectoring had meanwhile been making progress. The obvious approach was to mount swivelling engines which could thus be used to provide both lift and propulsion. In West Germany, Messerschmitt, Heinkel and Blohm formed a consortium which produced the VJ-101C, an experimental aircraft powered by six Rolls-Royce RB.145 engines, of which two were mounted in the fuselage for

Above: The VAK-191B combined two lift jets with a vectored thrust propulsion engine, a layout later used by the Yak-38 Forger.

Left: A German VTOL rig which used four RB.162 lift engines to explore the problems of V/STOL. Note the wind anemometer.

pure lift, while rotating wing-tip pods contained two each. The VJ-101C made its first free hover on 10 April 1963, and its first transition into level flight on 20 September. While it proved the viability of the system, exceeding Mach 1 on several occasions, it remained vulnerable to assymetric power loss, the more so as the rotating propulsion engines were located about as far from the centreline as it was possible to get. At the same time, swivelling pods housing engines for both lift and propulsion clearly imposes stringent limitations on the size of engines that can be used for this purpose.

While this project was not developed further, it formed the basis for another European consortium to produce the

VAK-191B, a subsonic fighter prototype with two lift jets and a single vectored thrust main jet. This was the format successfully used later by the Soviet Union for the Yak-38 Forger carrier fighter, but the VAK-191B was a late starter and did not transition from vertical to horizontal flight until 26 October 1972, by which time it had been overtaken by events. The programme was terminated at the end of that same year.

With the benefit of hindsight, it is obvious that the flat-riser is far superior to a tail-sitter. Equally obviously, it is easier to swivel the jet efflux than it is to swivel the entire engine. Nor was this a new idea. As far back as 1944, a German engineer, Herr von Wolff, had filed a patent for

jet deflection by using either a cascade, which is a lattice of moveable vanes, or by a segmented moveable jet pipe. Cascades were first used by the Bell X-14, which made its first transition on 24 May 1958. A fixed cascade first turned the thrust through 45deg; a second cascade rotated the thrust either straight down for lift, or aft for conventional flight. Whereas conventional fighters have their engines located well to the rear, the X-14 layout demanded that they be set forward, ahead of the centre of gravity, and this precluded development of an operational aircraft.

BRISTOL'S BE.53

The breakthrough for vectored thrust came from French aircraft designer Michel Wibault. Convinced that conventional airfields could all too easily be destroyed by nuclear weapons, he set himself the task of designing an aircraft suitable for off-base deployment. The result was his Gyroptère, a small flat-riser with a revolutionary thrust system. Completed in early-1956, it was powered by a single

History and Development

Bristol Orion turboshaft engine located in the rear fuselage. This drove a central shaft which was geared at right angles to four centrifugal blowers set in the sides of the aircraft. These were located ahead of the engine and athwart the centre of gravity. The blowers, rather similar in concept to the impellers of a centrifugal jet engine, were housed in snail shell-type casings which could be rotated through 90deg to produce either vertical lift or horizontal propulsion as the pilot so chose.

Having failed to interest either the French or American governments in his idea, Wibault approached the Mutual Weapons Development Programme (MWDP) team which was based in Paris. This organization had been set up to examine European military projects, and one of its greatest successes to date had been the British Bristol Orpheus turbojet which, while unwanted by its own country, had been selected to power every one of the competitors in the NATO Light Strike Fighter competition.

The head of the MWDP at that time was Colonel John Driscoll,

USAF. Since the proposed engine was the Orion, he passed the idea to Bristol Aero Engines for examination. Bristol's technical director, Sir Stanley Hooker, was at first not terribly impressed. The installation was heavy and complex, and the blowers inefficient. On the other hand, he was totally against the separate lift and thrust engine concept and favoured the use of a single engine to satisfy both

Below: Simplified drawings showing the evolution of the first Wibault-derived scheme, the BE.48, and how it evolved over a decade into the engine used to power the Harrier. The inlets to the gas generator on both the

BE.48 and BE.52/53 were actually at the top and bottom of the engine, and the front nozzles were on the sides. The green colour highlights the hot areas of each engine, while yellow shows the cooler areas.

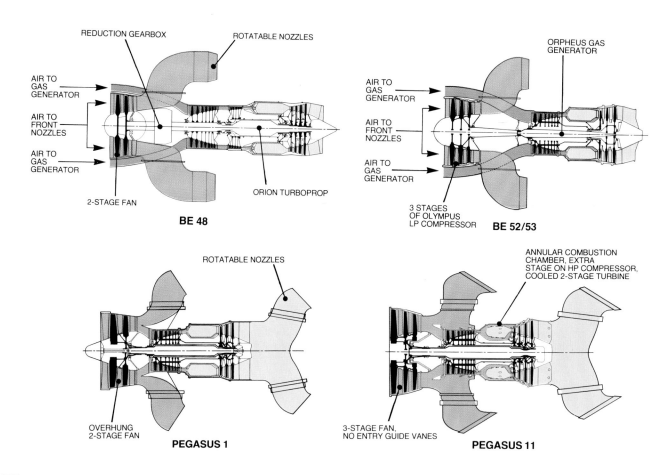

BE 48

BE 52/53

PEGASUS 1

PEGASUS 11

requirements. This being so, he agreed to carry out an appraisal of the project and assigned a small team to it.

The team of young engineers soon saw that better results could be achieved by replacing the clumsy blowers with swivelling elbow bends, feeding these with air from the engine itself. To produce high energy air at the front of the engine, they fitted a 1.5:1 reduction gearbox driving two stages from the low pressure compressor designed for the new Bristol Olympus turbojet. The compressor fan had a larger diameter than the engine, like the turbofans of today, and this provided thrust for the two swivelling nozzles in the front. In the early stages the rear nozzle remained standard.

This then, was the BE.48. The next step was to scrap the Orion in favour of the lighter and less complex Orpheus to produce the BE.52. Further development work led to the large front fan becoming an integral part of the engine, sharing a common inlet with the high pressure compressor. To minimize the gyroscopic effects of large masses rotating at high speeds — a potential cause of problems in hovering flight — the fan was made to contra-rotate against the high pressure spool. The result was the BE.53. Unlike many men who see their pet project transformed out of all recognition by others, Michel Wibault was

Left: Rear view of the Hawker P.1127 showing the original arrangement of the rearmost control valve system.

delighted with the developments, and shortly after became a joint patentee of a new VSTOL aircraft. In fact, plenum chamber burning (afterburning in chambers just inside the front nozzles) was mooted at this early stage, although it was put on the back burner for the time being.

PEGASUS AND P.1127

Hawker Aircraft was at this time one of the great names of British aviation, and they now entered the VSTOL scene quite by chance. Their legendary Chief Designer, Sir Sydney Camm, attended the 1957 Paris Air Show in company with Hawker's representative in France, Gerard Morel. Camm happened to mention that he was not exactly enchanted with the numerous lift jet schemes then being touted, and Morel, who quite fortuitously happened to be representing Bristol Aero Engines too, mentioned their work on the BE.53. The result was that, as

Above: Hawker P.1127 XP831 makes a conventional landing at RAE Bedford accompanied by a Hunter T.7 (left) chase aircraft.

Sir Stanley Hooker related on television many years later, he received a letter from Camm a few days later which simply said, "Dear Hooker, what are you doing about vertical take-off?" Shortly after, the first brochure for the BE.53 arrived on Camm's desk. He promptly turned it over to Senior Designer Ralph Hooper to see what he could make of it. By the end of June 1957, Hooper had produced an outline sketch of something looking vaguely like a Harrier, and Hooper received a phone call from Camm, asking "When are you coming to see me?" On enquiring what for, he got the dusty answer "About this lifting engine of yours, you bloody fool!" The show was on the road at last.

At this point the BE.53 still retained the conventional rear nozzle, and much of the engine thrust, which was never excessive, was being expelled horizontally, and was thus not available for lift. Again fortuitously, a

History and Development

Above: Three P.1127s in the early days of the project. From top to bottom, they are XP980, XP976 and XP831.

previous Hawker fighter, the Sea Hawk, designed in the days when engines had to be located amidships, had had a bifurcated nozzle as an alternative to a long efflux duct. It occured to Hooper that a similar arrangement would allow the hot end of the jet to be vectored also. This proposal was duly put to Bristol Aero Engines who approved it. At about this time, the BE.53 became known as the Pegasus. A brochure for a single seater VTOL attack aircraft, the P.1127, was prepared, and at the Farnborough Air Show in September of 1957 (when Paris and Farnborough were annual events) it was presented to Colonel Bill Chapman, who had succeeded John Driscoll as head of the MWDP team. While impressed, he pointed out that the range was inadequate for NATO requirements. More fuel was the answer, and fuel weighs heavy, so more power was needed. The Pegasus was upgraded (the first of

many times), in this case by including the high pressure compressor of the Orpheus 6. Also at this time, the clumsy elbow bends were replaced by shortened nozzles with cascade vanes. Another change was the use of bleed air from the hot end for the reaction control valves which gave control in the hover, and at low forward speeds. Previous to this it had been thought that cooler air from the fan would suffice, but calculations showed that the mass flow needed would demand enormous ducts.

Another problem to be overcome in the design period was where to stow the landing gear. The wing had to be set high in order to clear the rotating nozzles. To stow the gear in the wing would have needed inordinately long

main legs. Orthodox fuselage location was difficult due to the presence of the engine and nozzles. Finally it was decided to go for a bicycle gear layout with the main wheels on the centreline for and aft of the engine, and retractable outriggers on the wingtips. The wing was given a steep anhedral to reduce the outrigger length, but even then, Sir Sydney's dire prediction was that in the event of a heavy landing "they would snap like carrots". Fortunately in this matter he was wrong.

The first Pegasus engine ran in September 1959. It was rated at 9,000lb (40kN), and this was followed five months later by the 10,000lb (44.5kN) Pegasus 2. After a further six months work, this was raised by another 1,000lb (4kN), but the project was still looking marginal, especially in view of the fact that a significant fraction of the available thrust would be needed for the reaction control jets.

Normal running on a hard surface would mean that the exhaust gases would bounce back from it and be drawn into the intakes, with a consequent loss of thrust. To avoid this, a special grid was installed over a pit at Dunsfold airfield, in Surrey. The pit channelled the exhaust gases well away from the aeroplane. Everything possible was removed from the P.1127, in order to keep weight to an absolute minimum. With Chief Test Pilot Bill Bedford at the controls, tethered hovering trials commenced on 21 October 1960. It was not very spectacular. The P.1127 hopped, skidded, and slewed around the grid, a spectacle not exactly enhanced by the sight of Bill Bedford clambering out of the cockpit afterwards with one leg encased in plaster! The Pegasus 2's output was inadequate at this stage, and this showed in the lack of sufficient reaction control. The gaping inlets caused the P.1127 to weathercock, while the tethers inhibited free movement to a degree. But progress was made, available thrust was gradually increased, and on 19 November the first proper, i.e. untethered hovering flight was successfully accomplished.

THE KESTREL

After this, the first prototype was shifted to Royal Aircraft Establishment (RAE) Bedford where, on 13 March 1961, the first conventional flight was made. It was soon joined in the test programme by a second P.1127 prototype, and together they gradually explored the flight envelope. Complete transitions from the hover to forward flight and vice versa were first carried out on 12 September 1961. By the following month, the two P.1127s were operating from grass surfaces, and also demonstrating short rolling take-offs with the aid of the vectoring nozzles. Success was such that four P.1127 development aircraft were funded by the Ministry of Supply in November of that year, which only the previous June had first decided to support the project financially.

The development aircraft differed in detail from the originals; a kinked wing leading-edge, vortex generators on the upper wing surface, larger stabilators with greater anhedral, and inflatable rubber inlet lips were the outward signs. The first P.1127 was also brought up to the same standard, but in the meantime the second prototype had been lost when the left front nozzle came unglued in flight; Bill Bedford ejected successfully. But this apart, there seemed little prospect of a production run for a developed version, for the P.1127 could carry only a minimal warload for a short distance at firmly subsonic speeds. The trend at this time was for Mach 2 monsters, with Mach 3, 4 and even 5 on the horizon. To talk of subsonic fighters for the future smacked of heresy. All the while Rolls-Royce were trying hard to sell millions of lift engines around

Above: The Kestrel, pictured in March 1964, was the next stage of development. This view shows the inflatable rubber intake lips.

the world, and offering a convincing method of having one's cake and eating it; VTOL and Mach 2 as well! Confusion reigned in the minds of both the operational requirements staffs and the politicians who control the purse strings. What American defence analyst Pierre Sprey has called "Mach 2 Madness" exerted undue influence, and for years this was the chief obstacle to further development of what was to become the Harrier. The future of the little Hawker fighter seemed to depend entirely on how much thrust could be wrung from the Pegasus engine. Inevitably the idea of plenum chamber burning was revived in order to provide Mach 2 and all the other goodies. But this was to prove a red herring which obscured

the true worth of the thrust concept.

Rescue came from the usual source — the MWDP team in Paris. Larry Levy, a new arrival there, had the bright idea of putting together an experimental squadron so that the NATO air forces could actually evaluate the aircraft in the field. Equally important, he possessed the contacts to actually get something done. The result was the Tripartite Evaluation Squadron (TES), consisting of nine P.1127s and funded by Britain, the USA, and West Germany. This was eventually to save the idea of a subsonic STOVL attack fighter from oblivion because, being an international project, the British government could not easily cancel it. The new and improved aircraft, named Kestrel, were ordered in June 1962; the first flew on 7 March 1964, and the TES was formed just seven months later. At last the project was up and running!

AN RAF officer, who had best remain anonymous, once commented to the author that the Harrier looked as if someone had sat on it. By normal standards it is certainly an odd looking bird, although its appearance gives it an unusual operational advantage in that it provides a measure of aspect deception. At a distance, it is often difficult to tell exactly which way it is going and what it is doing.

The shape of a conventional combat aircraft is determined primarily by its role; what it is expected to carry; how far and how fast it is expected to go; and what it is expected to be able to do when it gets there. The aircraft is then designed as a series of compromises meeting these requirements to a greater or lesser degree. The engine(s) are located towards the rear; lots of heavy kit is stuck on up front to achieve a balance, and the weights which vary in flight, such as ordnance and fuel, are clustered around the centre of gravity in the middle. With the Harrier, the overriding need was to have the thrust acting through the centre of gravity for vertical flight and hovering. The two front nozzles had

therefore to be placed ahead of the centre of gravity and the two rear nozzles astern of it. Consequently, the Pegasus engine had to be located well forward by conventional design stan-

Below: XP836, the second prototype, was lost when the left front fibreglass engine nozzle came unglued in flight.

Above: The huge "elephant's ear" intakes are sized for thrust at full throttle and low speed.

dards, and the basic aircraft had to be designed around it. Only after this stage could the airframe be "tweaked" to suit the mission requirements, and these were inevitably limited by weight if STOVL requirements were to be met.

One of the more obvious characteristics of the Harrier is its large "elephant-ear" intakes. The distance between the intake lip and the face of the fan is very short by any standards, and the intakes are sized for thrust at full throttle at low speeds; they are considerably larger than would be needed for economical cruise. The inlets were difficult to optimize for the mission spectrum; early experiments were conducted with inflatable rubber lips to enable a change to be made from a blunt to a sharp edge, but it was found that these were impossible

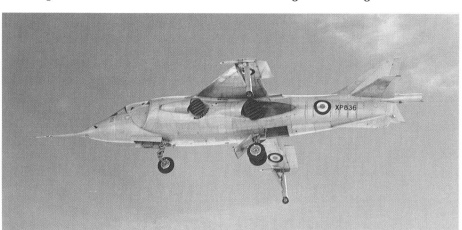

XP836

to keep serviceable. The final answer was to have a lip of moderate radius, with eight auxiliary doors forming an almost complete semi-circle. The large intakes had one advantage, however. They enabled the forward cascaded nozzles to be located behind them, thus eliminating most of the profile drag which would have been caused had they projected into the slipstream.

Vectoring the thrust is achieved by means of a single lever in the cockpit which acts in exactly the same way as the throttle: it pushes forward for acceleration and forward flight, and pulls back to decelerate and hover. The nozzles, which must move in unison, pivot through 98.5deg in all at a rate of up to 100deg/sec. This allows a modicum of reverse thrust to be used to decelerate the aircraft ready for the hover. It also permits the Harrier to fly backwards, which aids precision landing. This has often been demonstrated in Harrier flying displays. Back in 1978, the author attended a rehearsal at Royal Air Force (RAF) Wittering for a demonstration for General Allen, the then USAF Chief-of-Staff. A pilot from No. 1 (Fighter) Squadron, RAF, actually climbed his

Below: While the Harrier can operate from grass fields, ground erosion is a problem.

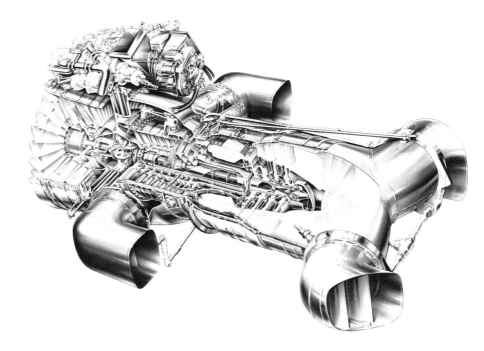

Above: The Pegasus 11 engine seen with elbow rather than cascade-type front nozzles.

Harrier backwards at an angle of about 20deg!

When the nozzles reach an angle of about 20deg from the horizontal, high pressure bleed air at up to 180lb/sq in (12.41 bars) and 400°C is released into the reaction control system. This allows the Harrier to be controlled at low speeds and in the hover. The puffer ducts are located beneath the nose and the tail for pitch control; on either side of the tail for yaw control; and on the wing-tips for roll. The wing-tip valves vary from the others in that they can direct air either up or down, giving high authority control. Early Harriers were reputed to be a bit "twitchy" at certain angles of bank, but this is now regarded as a thing of the past. The valves themselves are linked to the orthodox flight controls, and the pilot flies the aircraft with stick and rudder in the normal way.

THE WING

The wing of the Harrier is small at 201sq ft (18.67m²), the sweep angle is moderate, and the wing loading fairly high. In later versions such as the GR.5/AV-8B the span and area were both increased, but this is running

Developing the Breed

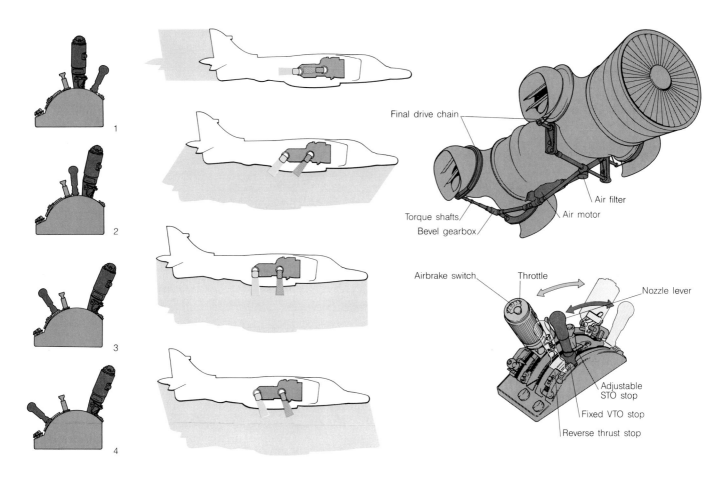

Final drive chain

Torque shafts

Bevel gearbox

Air filter

Air motor

Airbrake switch

Throttle

Nozzle lever

Adjustable STO stop

Fixed VTO stop

Reverse thrust stop

ahead of our story. An attack aircraft spends much of its time flying at high speed in the bumpy air at low level. This tends to give the pilot an uncomfortable ride which can be fatiguing over quite short periods, and potentially reduces his weaponeering accuracy. To minimize this effect, the wing loading needs to be on the high side in order to keep gust response low. On the other hand, manoeuvrability over the target is needed, and high wing loadings militate against this.

The Harrier wing is a *tour de force*. A STOVL aircraft wing is not dictated by runway performance requirements, and so no heavy and complex high-lift devices were needed. Neither was there a supersonic level speed requirement,

Above: A major advantage of the Harrier is that it has only one extra cockpit control, a nozzle lever (right, in red). The limits of the nozzle angle are set by two fixed stops and an STO stop set by the pilot, usually 55deg. The sequence (left) shows how the direction of the thrust vector is controlled by the nozzle lever while the throttle controls engine speed and hence the length of

and so the wing could be optimized for subsonic cruise. The design team opted for very high aerodynamic lift, selecting a blunt leading-edge section and a thickness/chord ratio varying between 10 per cent at the root and

the thrust vector. 1 shows normal cruising flight, and 3 full power as used in the hover; 2 shows the transition between them, and 4 reverse thrust with the nozzles at 15deg forward. All four nozzles must rotate in exact unison (top right) to ensure success; bleed air drives a motor geared to them via rotary shafts and chains, the nozzles rotating in special non-stick bearings.

five per cent at the tip. A small dogtooth was incorporated on the inboard leading-edge, and a row of 12 vortex generators was added to the upper surface. At 460mph (741km/h) Indicated Air Speed (IAS) the wing generates an average lift exceeding 430lb/sq ft (2,098kg/m²) over the gross area. Although in this flight condition (Angle of Attack [AoA] exceeding 20deg) the wing is in the zone of heavy buffeting, there is a complete absence of pitch-up, wing drop, or any other handling problem. Nor are any vices evident when the Harrier is dived at supersonic speeds. The wing design allows a very simple structure to be used which, divested of mechanical components such as hydraulic jacks etc, weighs less than if it were carved from the heavier grades of balsa wood!

The wing, which is constructed in a single piece, is mounted over the engine compartment, and has to be removed for an engine change. As noted in the previous chapter, this high-set postion has inevitably meant that a steep anhedral angle must be employed in order to keep the wing-tip outriggers to a reasonable length. It is also a major contributor to the Harrier's unorthodox appearance. The final interesting feature is the ferry tip, which can be bolted on, giving a greater span and increased range, although flight load limits are reduced by about 50 per cent when this is fitted. The ferry tip, which is 2ft 3in (69cm) long, can be attached by two men in less than one hour, and gives roughly a nine per cent range increment for a given fuel weight. To achieve this increase in combat configuration, an extra weight of fuel would have to be carried, amounting to 50 times the weight of the ferry tips themselves.

EARLY REFINEMENTS

Of its very nature, STOVL implies dispersed basing. As noted in the previous chapter, a bicycle landing gear configuration had to be adopted with wing outriggers. Tyre pressures on the Harrier are 90lb/sq in (6.20

Above: A GR.1 fires at a ground target with 68mm unguided rockets, its wing sturdy despite the force exerted on it.

Left: Three Harrier GR.3s carry a mixture of SNEB rocket pods and fuel tanks on their underwing and centreline pylons.

bars) on the main gears and 95lb/sq in (6.55 bars) on the outriggers. This is far less than those of conventional aircraft, where 300lb/sq in (20.70 bars) is fairly typical, and allows the Harrier to move freely over relatively soft ground. Should it start to bog down, a bit of nozzle and a touch of throttle soon have it under way again. In the

Developing the Breed

surfaces. Where the steerable nose-wheel failed to grip, a touch of nozzle would activate the puffers which would give adequate directional control.

The tail surfaces are of orthodox construction and layout. The shape of the fin and rudder owe at least something to the Hawker Hunter, while the all-moving, one-piece stabilators have, like the wing, a steep anhedral angle. A small ventral fin is also incorporated. This carries a bumper to protect the rear end in the event of an injudicious landing. While this also adds to stability at high AoA there is no doubt that it helps the aircraft to look ''right''.

The cockpit is small, and in all early Harriers, the canopy is set flush with the top of the fuselage. This severely restricts the view aft, a fact which is not helped by the large intakes set close on either side. Only when the Harrier was considered for air combat in the form of the Sea Harrier was the seating position raised and a bubble canopy installed; a trend followed by the later GR.5 and AV-8B. Avionics were simple; a Ferranti inertial nav/attack system formed the basis, with a moving-map display showing the position of the aircraft at all times. No radar was included; it was not deemed necessary for the close air support (CAS) mission, and without a redesign

Below: The GR.5's moving-map display in the centre is the heart of the nav/attack sytsem.

early squadron days, problems were encountered during orthodox (i.e. horizontal) landings, and some most spectacular skids were recorded, although the flimsy-looking outriggers stood up well to the strain. Normal operational use, however, dictates the use of vertical landings, the normal sink rate of which is less than 8ft/sec (2.44m/sec). The gear is actually stressed for a sink rate half as great

Above: A group of six two-seat T.2 trainers with a ventral fin, stretched fuselage and larger tail.

again as this. For technical reasons, the ride of the Harrier over bumpy and undulating surfaces is considerably better than that of a conventional machine with a tricycle landing gear. Also, an unexpected bonus was discovered when taxying on very icy it would have been very difficult to find somewhere to house it. A Tactical Air Navigation (TACAN) unit and a gyrocompass were installed, along with a Smiths Industries Head-Up Display (HUD), Radar Warning Receiver (RWR), Identification Friend or Foe (IFF), and radios covering the High Frequency (HF), Very High Frequency (VHF) and Ultra High Frequency (UHF) communication bands. Harriers were later fitted with a laser ranger, giving rise to the familiar "Snoopy Nose". The pilot sat on a Martin Baker zero/zero ejection seat, and above him the canopy was fitted with a detonating chord. Whereas in conventional flight the canopy would be whisked away astern by the slipstream when jettisoned, in the hover it would just go straight up, followed a split second later by the pilot. A large and heavy transparency, it was a potential source of serious injury as the pilot ascended vertically on his ejection seat. The detonating chord would fragment the canopy into small and less lethal pieces.

The normal procedure with fast jets is to design a two-seater conversion trainer alongside the operational aircraft. In the case of the Harrier, early conversion training in the RAF was done with single seaters, a fact that speaks volumes for the easy, vice-free handling of the type. To a lesser degree it reflected the lack of available power; a two seater is intrinsically heavier than its single seat counterpart. The need was clear and as greater potential was wrung out of the Pegasus engine, a development contract for just such a two-seater was issued in 1967. The task was made more difficult by the requirement for it to be made fully operational, enabling it to be flown with a full load of fuel and weapons

Right: HUD presentation during a simulated attack run as seen from the rear seat of a T-bird.

Developing the Breed

Left: The addition of a Ferranti Laser Ranger/Marked Target Seeker created a new profile — the ''Snoopy Nose'' of the GR.3.

in time of war if need be.

The first consideration was the seat layout. Bearing in mind that the centre of gravity had still to match the centre of thrust, it might have been simpler to adopt a side-by-side seating arrangement, as Hawker Siddeley had done with the earlier Hunter, but this would have involved a much wider front fuselage causing consequent problems with the engine intakes. One or two really eccentric solutions were proposed, such as placing the instructor's cockpit just ahead of the fin, but realistically it was Hobson's Choice; a tandem seat layout. This was achieved by slicing off the front cockpit and inserting a plug containing the second seat behind it. Various pieces of kit were moved, including the air conditioning system and the inertial platform, and the rear of the enlarged cockpit was located over the nosewheel bay. This had the beneficial effect of raising it by some 18in (46cm), giving the back-seater a good view ahead. The canopy was side-hinged.

The extended nose naturally had a destabilizing effect which could only be offset by greater keel area. This was provided by moving the tail further aft and enlarging the dorsal fin. A larger ventral fin was also fitted, its shape changed to resemble those of the Grumman F-14 Tomcat carrier borne fighter. The tail cone was extended and ballasted to restore the centre of gravity to its rightful place, and finally, the front and rear pitch control puffers were extended fore and aft respectively, and the yaw control

Left: G-VTOL, BAe's two-seat civil demonstrator, raising dust clouds while making a short rolling landing.

Right: A very clear view of the Ferranti 106 LR/MTS with test instrumentation installed. It also shows the poor view rearward.

Above: Nos 3 and 4 Sqns with Harriers are based in Germany. This GR.1 of 3 Sqn overflies the rebuilt Moehne Dam in the Ruhr.

puffers were extended aft, thus increasing the moment arm. Various stability problems were encountered, but these were gradually overcome.

For conversion training, the pupil takes the front seat with the instructor behind him. Flown operationally as a single seater, the second seat is removed, as is the ballast in the tailcone. For overseas deployments it is quite normal for a ''T-bird'' to accompany the single-seaters, and it is invariably flown by the detachment commander.

THE first production Harrier GR.1 flew on 28 December 1967. It had been clear from the outset that any improved variants would depend on obtaining ever more thrust from the Pegasus engine, and the main efforts were concentrated in this direction. Improved water injection, and combustion chamber cooling; an increased capacity fuel pump; and improved cooling to the turbine blades, which permitted higher turbine entry temperatures to be used, produced the Pegasus 102, which was rated at 20,500lb st (91.20kN) a useful advance over the 19,000lb st (84.50kN) of the Pegasus 101. The 102 entered production in 1969, and was retrofitted to serving GR.1s, which then became GR.1As. The Pegasus 102 also powered the two-seat Harrier T.2.

Below: A line-up of No 3 Sqn GR.3s in Germany all fitted with RWR aerials in their fin edges.

HARRIER GR.3

Further engine improvements produced the Pegasus 103, with mass flow increased by reblading the fan; even higher turbine temperatures; a revised combustion chamber; and a manual fuel control system. The Pegasus 103 was to become the standard service engine, and aircraft powered by it became Harrier GR.3s. Of course, it was not just the engine that was being upgraded; various other small modifications were made, but these were generally of an engineering nature, and unrelated to performance or combat capability.

The one real exception came a short while later. This was the Ferranti Type 106 Laser Ranger and Marked Target Seeker (LRMTS) which was housed in the nose. An aid to accurate attack on ground targets, interfaced with the rest of the nav/attack system, it operates in two modes. In the first,

it is pointed at a target directly ahead, or within 20deg of the aircraft centreline, and is stabilized to automatically stay on target. On command, it shoots out pulses of laser light; from these it obtains very accurate data on range, rate of closure, and angles, presenting the figures to the pilot on the HUD. The second mode is passive. It automatically searches for laser-designated targets marked by friendly ground forces, and having found one, it locks onto it and presents the target position and attack information on the HUD.

First tested in 1970, the Ferranti 106 LRMTS commenced retrofitting to Harrier GR.3s in the middle of the decade, and was new-build equipment by 1976. All RAF Harriers were subsequently to carry it, housed in a lengthened nose thimble (the "Snoopy Nose" referred to earlier), which spoilt the rather cute look of the early Harrier models and added to the off-beat shape of the aircraft. Oddly, the new nose had no noticeable adverse effects on handling.

Above: The Kestrel, designated the XV-6A, undergoes USMC suitability evaluations in 1966 aboard CV-62 USS *Independence*.

Another addition at about this time was an RWR, the forward-and rear-looking aerials of which were located in a fairing near the top of the fin leading-edge, and the extreme rear of the tailcone, respectively. Very basic in concept, the RWR merely warns the pilot from which quadrant a hostile radar is looking at him from. The power demands of these two pieces of kit resulted in a new 12kVA alternator replacing the two 4kVA units of earlier Harriers.

McDONNELL DOUGLAS AV-8

Very similar to the early GR.3 but without the LRMTS, is the American AV-8A. The United States Marine Corps (USMC) had been interested in the Harrier almost from its inception, and had a firm requirement for organic air cover for amphibious operations. Rotary wing airpower was demonstrably inadequate, but VTOL or STOVL would fill their needs admirably. Surprisingly, the USMC had taken no part in the Kestrel TES, although the US Army had. After the

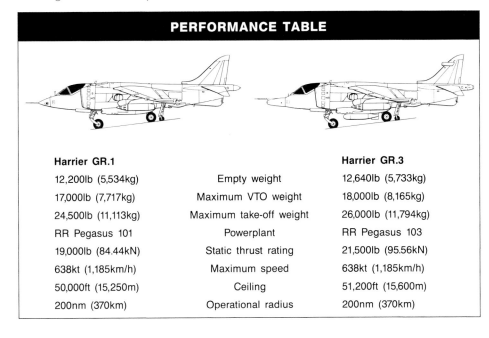

PERFORMANCE TABLE

Harrier GR.1		Harrier GR.3
12,200lb (5,534kg)	Empty weight	12,640lb (5,733kg)
17,000lb (7,717kg)	Maximum VTO weight	18,000lb (8,165kg)
24,500lb (11,113kg)	Maximum take-off weight	26,000lb (11,794kg)
RR Pegasus 101	Powerplant	RR Pegasus 103
19,000lb (84.44kN)	Static thrust rating	21,500lb (95.56kN)
638kt (1,185km/h)	Maximum speed	638kt (1,185km/h)
50,000ft (15,250m)	Ceiling	51,200ft (15,600m)
200nm (370km)	Operational radius	200nm (370km)

Top: GR.3s of No 4 Sqn carrying multi-sensor pods on the centreline for reconnaissance.

Above: A temporary arctic paint scheme worn by a No 1 Sqn GR.1 deployed to Bardufoss, Norway.

trials had ended, six Kestrels had been shipped to the USA where they had been redesignated XV-6A, and some eventually arrived at the Naval Air Test Center (NATC) at Patuxent River, Maryland, where the USMC finally got their hands on them. In April 1966, a Kestrel was flown from the commando assault ship USS *Raleigh*, a vessel too small to operate conventional fixed-wing aircraft, and this clearly showed the aircraft's potential. But in spite of this the Kestrel was

The Variants

not really a combat-capable aircraft, and only with the emergence of the more powerful and developed Harrier did the possibility look like becoming a reality. Then, at the Farnborough Air Show in September 1968, three USMC officers turned up at the Hawker Siddeley chalet and asked to fly the Harrier! They were granted ten flights each, and the rest is history. The USMC had to have it!

It being virtually impossible to sell

Above: This AV-8A of VMFA-513 was the second one to be built and was delivered in 1971. It is seen here on the USS _Guam_.

foreign military aircraft to the United States, a deal was concluded with McDonnell Douglas at St. Louis, Missouri, for licence manufacture, while Pratt & Whitney teamed with Rolls-Royce (who had since bought out Bristol Aero Engines) for the Pegasus,

which was to be designated F402-RR in USMC service. As originally specified, the AV-8A was to be powered by the Pegasus 103 (F400-RR-401) as fitted to the GR.3, but as this was not ready in time, the first ten aircraft were powered by the earlier 102s. The Martin Baker IXD ejection seat was replaced by the indigenous Stencel SIII-S3, and American radios and IFF were also fitted. The other changes mainly concerned weapon delivery, the USMC mission being rather different to that of the RAF. The two 30mm (1.18in) Aden cannon were at first regarded as provisional, but their reliability and effectiveness was such that they were retained. Wiring for AIM-9 Sidewinder air-to-air missiles (AAM) was installed, so that one of these self-defence weapons could be carried on each outer pylon. A Smiths Industries HUD and multi-mode weapons aiming computer was fitted for air-to-surface weapon delivery; among other things this included the Continuously Computed Impact Point, (CCIP, or "Death Dot"), which showed where

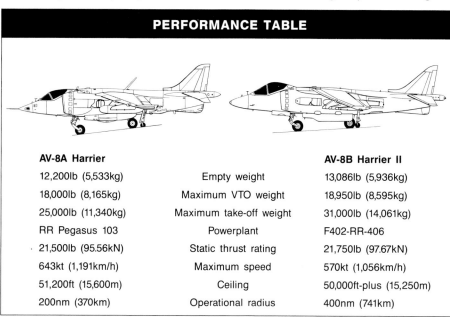

PERFORMANCE TABLE

AV-8A Harrier		AV-8B Harrier II
12,200lb (5,533kg)	Empty weight	13,086lb (5,936kg)
18,000lb (8,165kg)	Maximum VTO weight	18,950lb (8,595kg)
25,000lb (11,340kg)	Maximum take-off weight	31,000lb (14,061kg)
RR Pegasus 103	Powerplant	F402-RR-406
21,500lb (95.56kN)	Static thrust rating	21,750lb (97.67kN)
643kt (1,191km/h)	Maximum speed	570kt (1,056km/h)
51,200ft (15,600m)	Ceiling	50,000ft-plus (15,250m)
200nm (370km)	Operational radius	400nm (741km)

Above: A test of the Stencel SIII-S3 ejection seat which the USMC preferred for the AV-8.

Above: An AV-8A in a hover; its successor AV-8B has a multi-function cockpit display (right).

the weapons would impact at any given moment. Whereas the RAF Harrier was intended to make a first-pass strike, its USMC counterpart expected to make multiple attacks during a single mission. The USMC also wanted a rough-and-ready nav/attack system which would require no warm-up and alignment time, thus reducing reaction delays, and which would also minimize the need for skilled maintenance.

Between 1975 and 1984, most of the surviving AV-8As underwent a comprehensive update, to emerge as AV-8Cs. This involved a structural programme aimed at extending the airframe fatigue life to 4,000 hours, while Lift Improvement Devices (LID) as designed for the AV-8B were fitted to enhance the warload. Most of the other improvements involve avionics; a modern electronic warfare (EW) suite; secure voice communications; chaff and flare dispensers; better UHF radios etc. An On-Board Oxygen Generator System (OBOGS), is also fitted. This cuts out the need to continually replace oxygen bottles, with a consequent easing of logistic problems.

SEA HARRIER FRS.1

Meanwhile, Britain's Royal Navy had been doing some careful thinking. In 1966, the Labour government of the day had decided to terminate the Navy's fixed-wing capability, and cancel the new carrier which was to have replaced HMS *Ark Royal*. Air protection for the Fleet was now to be provided by the RAF! Without a big carrier, the fast jet at sea was a non-starter. Then in 1968, the powers-that-be settled for building helicopter carriers, which were to be known as

"through deck cruisers". This new class was so obviously a "Harrier Carrier", that it popularly became known as the "see-through cruiser!".

In February 1963, Bill Bedford had landed a P.1127 on the deck of HMS *Ark Royal*, and since that time, Kestrels, Harriers and AV-8As had operated from ships, some of them quite small, with no real difficulty. The main problem was one of attitude. Mach 2 was fashionable, and a very strong case could be made for it being essential for the Fleet air defence role. The Harrier was firmly subsonic in level flight, as well as being range and warload limited. Yet finally common-sense prevailed, and in January 1973 an order was placed for a sea-going variant based very closely on the GR.3. This was to emerge as the Sea Harrier FRS.1, although first flight was delayed until 20 August 1978. This was a production model; it

Below: The Sea Harrier FRS.1 was developed from the GR.3 with a revised cockpit. Here it is seen in its low-visibility paint.

had been agreed that a prototype would not be necessary.

The Sea Harrier FRS.1 differed from the GR.3 mainly at the front end. The first essential was to fit a multi-mode air intercept radar. This, combined with new nav/attack kit, demanded more display area than existed in the GR.3, and was the primary reason for the cockpit being raised about 11in (28cm). Rearward view from the cockpit of a GR.3 is poor, and sideways, past the large intakes, not a lot better. Raising the cockpit on the Sea Harrier gave a great improvement to the all-round view, which is most essential for the air combat role. At the same time, the canopy was bulged to give a better view forwards and downwards.

The radar chosen was the Ferranti *Blue Fox*, which was housed in a completely redesigned nose. This had four main modes, which was not a lot when one compares it to the nearly contemporary Hughes APG-65, but it was a small and light package. The modes were Search, Attack (which divided into air/air and air/surface), and Boresight for targets of opportunity. With no Doppler facility it had no real look-down capability, but as its primary mission was to intercept Soviet long-range reconnaissance and missile-carrying aircraft, this was, like the lack of supersonic speed, thought not to matter a great deal.

In terms of avionics, the Sea Harrier had little in common with the GR.3, and the cockpit displays were completely redesigned in consequence. The increased depth caused by raising the cockpit was compensated for by increasing the height of the fin by 4in (10cm), at the same time building in the RWR. Turbulence caused by the carrier superstructure demanded increased roll control in the hover, and the reaction control valves in the wings were increased in diameter; mooring lugs were added to the nose gear leg;

and the horizontal stabilizer travel slightly increased. The yaw vane was set centrally instead of being offset as in the GR.3. Other changes were all under the skin. The pilot sits on an improved zero/zero ejection seat. His work load is high, especially with the radar in use, and to ease this, an autopilot gives automatic holds for direction, altitude, and turn rate. A 15kVA alternator was fitted to supply the extra power required by the radar and avionics, together with an uprated gearbox. The aircraft and engine were

Left: Two FRS.1s of No 899 Sqn demonstrate the close formation hover above a carrier-deck.

navalized by using an alloy less susceptible to salt water corrosion, to produce the Pegasus 104.

Meanwhile, the most remarkable addition to Sea Harrier capability had been developed. Normal Harrier landings are vertical, but a short rolling take-off is used to maximize their payload. Lieutenant Commander Douglas Taylor, RN, now came up with an idea so simple that many thought that it couldn't possibly work. He calculated that if the Harrier left the ground at an angle, the upward velocity vector would compensate the downward pull of gravity for long enough to allow normal flying speed to build up. In practice this would

Below: The Sea Harrier cockpit with basic flight instruments replacing the moving-map.

mean that either a greater load could be carried, or a shorter take-off run used. An added bonus was that when launching from a ship in heavy weather, the aircraft would be pointing up away from the water, even when the bow was on a downswing. It was tried; it worked; and the ski jump is now a familiar feature of the Royal Navy's carrier force.

Left: An airborne formation of FRS.1s in 1981 from No 801 Sqn (HMS *Heron*), top, No 800 Sqn (HMS *Hermes*), centre, and No 899 Sqn (HMS *Invincible*).

Below: A well armed FRS.2, its nose radome contains enhanced radar capability and combined with its four AIM-120 missiles makes it a formidable opponent.

SEA HARRIER FRS.2

The South Atlantic conflict of 1982 conclusively demonstrated that the Royal Navy could get involved in wars other than a NATO/WarPac confrontation; but it also exposed several shortcomings in the FRS.1. The main ones were an inadequate radar and a lack of a true look-down capability; the lack of a medium-range weapon; and lack of combat persistence. In the latter case it was often found that when Argentinian aircraft were encountered, two AIM-9L Sidewinders were not

enough for the number of targets. This was quickly remedied, and FRS.1s now carry four such AAMs. The other points were more difficult to remedy, and in 1984 an upgrade to FRS.2 standards was planned, with new-build aircraft following on later.

The Sea Harrier FRS.2 first flew on 19 September, 1989. It carries the Ferranti *Blue Vixen* coherent, pulse Doppler, multi-mode radar; much longer ranged and more capable than *Blue Fox*, and with a true look-down capability. Combined with the AIM-120 Advanced Medium-Range Air-to-Air Missile (AMRAAM), this will give the FRS.2 a head-on, beyond visual range kill capability. Four AMRAAMs will be carried, or two AMRAAMs and four Sidewinders.

Externally, the FRS.2 is not very different. The fuselage has been extended by 13¾in (35cm), which gives extra space for avionics, and 8in (20cm) wing-tip extensions were proposed to keep the centre of lift within limits when AMRAAM is carried, although it has been found that they are not needed. The radome is larger and less pointed. One significant omission is the ram air turbine, used to provide control power in the event of an engine failure.

The cockpit has been totally redesigned to reduce pilot workload. Hands On Throttle And Stick (HOTAS) controls have been adopted, together with multi-function displays. Improved nav/attack kit will be fitted, as will the Guardian RWR, which can identify most threats by comparing them with a stored library of 200 radar signatures. In all, the FRS.2 is now much more "user-friendly".

Left: The innovative ski-jump used with vectored thrust allows short take off at high weights.

The Variants

McDonnell-Douglas/ British Aerospace Harrier GR.5 cutaway drawing key

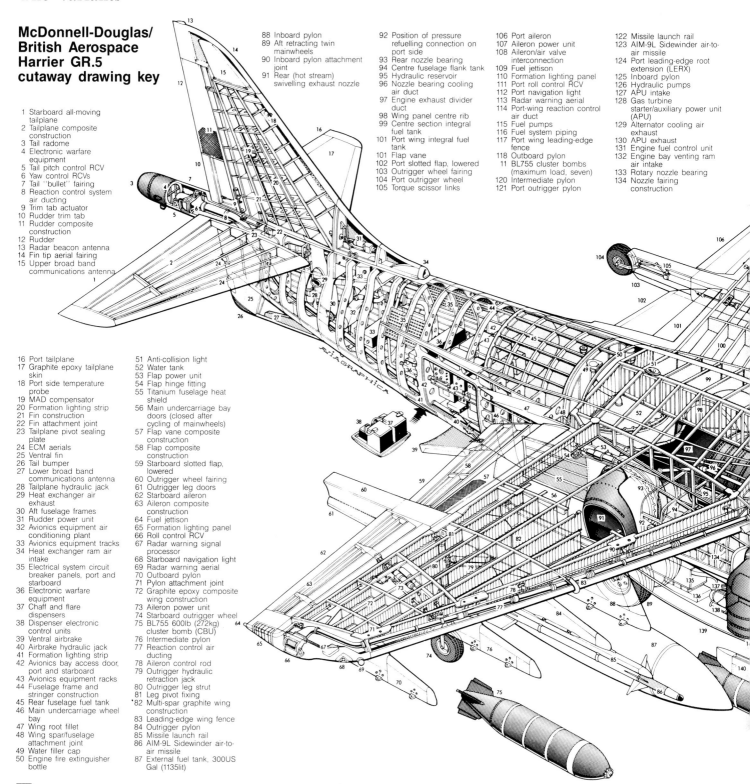

1 Starboard all-moving tailplane
2 Tailplane composite construction
3 Tail radome
4 Electronic warfare equipment
5 Tail pitch control RCV
6 Yaw control RCVs
7 Tail "bullet" fairing
8 Reaction control system air ducting
9 Trim tab actuator
10 Rudder trim tab
11 Rudder composite construction
12 Rudder
13 Radar beacon antenna
14 Fin tip aerial fairing
15 Upper broad band communications antenna

16 Port tailplane
17 Graphite epoxy tailplane skin
18 Port side temperature probe
19 MAD compensator
20 Formation lighting strip
21 Fin construction
22 Fin attachment joint
23 Tailplane pivot sealing plate
24 ECM aerials
25 Ventral fin
26 Tail bumper
27 Lower broad band communications antenna
28 Tailplane hydraulic jack
29 Heat exchanger air exhaust
30 Aft fuselage frames
31 Rudder power unit
32 Avionics equipment air conditioning plant
33 Avionics equipment tracks
34 Heat exchanger ram air intake
35 Electrical system circuit breaker panels, port and starboard
36 Electronic warfare equipment
37 Chaff and flare dispensers
38 Dispenser electronic control units
39 Ventral airbrake
40 Airbrake hydraulic jack
41 Formation lighting strip
42 Avionics bay access door, port and starboard
43 Avionics equipment racks
44 Fuselage frame and stringer construction
45 Rear fuselage fuel tank
46 Main undercarriage wheel bay
47 Wing root fillet
48 Wing spar/fuselage attachment joint
49 Water filler cap
50 Engine fire extinguisher bottle

51 Anti-collision light
52 Water tank
53 Flap power unit
54 Flap hinge fitting
55 Titanium fuselage heat shield
56 Main undercarriage bay doors (closed after cycling of mainwheels)
57 Flap vane composite construction
58 Flap composite construction
59 Starboard slotted flap, lowered
60 Outrigger wheel fairing
61 Outrigger leg doors
62 Starboard aileron
63 Aileron composite construction
64 Fuel jettison
65 Formation lighting panel
66 Roll control RCV
67 Radar warning signal processor
68 Starboard navigation light
69 Radar warning aerial
70 Outboard pylon
71 Pylon attachment joint
72 Graphite epoxy composite wing construction
73 Aileron power unit
74 Starboard outrigger wheel
75 BL755 600lb (272kg) cluster bomb (CBU)
76 Intermediate pylon
77 Reaction control air ducting
78 Aileron control rod
79 Outrigger hydraulic retraction jack
80 Outrigger leg strut
81 Leg pivot fixing
82 Multi-spar graphite wing construction
83 Leading-edge wing fence
84 Outrigger pylon
85 Missile launch rail
86 AIM-9L Sidewinder air-to-air missile
87 External fuel tank, 300US Gal (1135lit)

88 Inboard pylon
89 Aft retracting twin mainwheels
90 Inboard pylon attachment joint
91 Rear (hot stream) swivelling exhaust nozzle
92 Position of pressure refuelling connection on port side
93 Rear nozzle bearing
94 Centre fuselage flank tank
95 Hydraulic reservoir
96 Nozzle bearing cooling air duct
97 Engine exhaust divider duct
98 Wing panel centre rib
99 Centre section integral fuel tank
100 Port wing integral fuel tank
101 Flap vane
102 Port slotted flap, lowered
103 Outrigger wheel fairing
104 Port outrigger wheel
105 Torque scissor links

106 Port aileron
107 Aileron power unit
108 Aileron/air valve interconnection
109 Fuel jettison
110 Formation lighting panel
111 Port roll control RCV
112 Port navigation light
113 Radar warning aerial
114 Port-wing reaction control air duct
115 Fuel pumps
116 Fuel system piping
117 Port wing leading-edge fence
118 Outboard pylon
11 BL755 cluster bombs (maximum load, seven)
120 Intermediate pylon
121 Port outrigger pylon

122 Missile launch rail
123 AIM-9L Sidewinder air-to-air missile
124 Port leading-edge root extension (LERX)
125 Inboard pylon
126 Hydraulic pumps
127 APU intake
128 Gas turbine starter/auxiliary power unit (APU)
129 Alternator cooling air exhaust
130 APU exhaust
131 Engine fuel control unit
132 Engine bay venting ram air intake
133 Rotary nozzle bearing
134 Nozzle fairing construction

135 Ammunition tank, 110 rounds
136 Cartridge case collector box
137 Ammunition feed chute
138 Fuel vent
139 Gun pack strake
140 Fuselage centreline pylon
141 Zero scarf forward (fan air) nozzle
142 Ventral gun pack (two)
143 Aden 25mm cannon
144 Engine drain mast
145 Hydraulic system ground connectors
146 Forward fuselage flank fuel tank
147 Engine electronic control units
148 Engine accessory equipment gearbox

149 Gearbox driven alternator
150 Rolls-Royce Pegasus 11 Mk 105 vectored thrust turbofan
151 Formation lighting strips
152 Engine oil tank
153 Bleed air spill duct
154 Air conditioning intake scoops
155 Cockpit air conditioning system heat exchanger
156 Engine compressor/fan face
157 Heat exchanger discharge to intake duct
158 Nose undercarriage hydraulic retraction jack
159 Intake blow-in doors
160 Engine bay venting air scoop
161 Cannon muzzle fairing
162 Lift augmentation retractable cross-dam
163 Cross-dam hydraulic jack
164 Nosewheel
165 Nosewheel forks
166 Landing/taxiing lamp
167 Retractable boarding step
168 Nosewheel doors (closed after cycling of undercarriage)
169 Nosewheel door jack

170 Boundary layer bleed air duct
171 Nose undercarriage wheel bay
172 Kick-in boarding steps
173 Cockpit rear pressure bulkhead
174 Starboard side console panel
175 Martin-Baker Mk 10 ejection seat
176 Safety harness
177 Ejection seat headrest
178 Port engine air intake
179 Probe hydraulic jack
180 Retractable inflight-refuelling probe (bolt-on pack)
181 Cockpit canopy cover
182 Miniature detonating cord (MDC) canopy breaker
183 Canopy frame
184 Engine throttle and nozzle control levers
185 Pilot's head-up-display (HUD)
186 Instrument panel
187 Moving map display
188 Control column
189 Central warning system panel
190 Cockpit pressure floor

191 Underfloor control runs
192 Formation lighting strips
193 Aileron trim actuator
194 Rudder pedals
195 Cockpit section composite construction
196 Instrument panel shroud
197 One-piece wrap-around windscreen panel
198 Ram air intake (cockpit fresh air)
199 Front pressure bulkhead
200 Incidence vane
201 Air data computer
202 Pilot tube
203 Lower IFF aerial
204 Nose pitch control air valve
205 Pitch trim control actuator
206 Electrical system equipment
207 Yaw vane
208 Upper IFF aerial
209 Electronic warfare equipment
210 ARBS head exchanger
211 MIRLS sensors
212 Hughes Angle Rate Bombing System (ARBS)
213 Composite construction nose cone
214 ARBS glazed aperture

AV-8B & GR.5/7 HARRIER II

From the early 1970s, moves were afoot to increase the Harrier's capability. Both BAe Kingston Division, (as Hawker Siddeley had now become), and McDonnell Douglas prepared studies for advanced Harriers.

Meanwhile, McDonnell Douglas studies had shown that payload range could be doubled, i.e. the same load for twice the distance or double the load for the same distance, by simply modifying the airframe, for a slight penalty in maximum speed. At the same time, BAe Kingston was working on the "big wing" Harrier for the RAF, who wanted the next variant to have a worthwhile air combat capability, with a sustained turn rate of 20deg/sec. The other RAF requirement was that their existing GR.3s should be capable of being upgraded to the new standard. The politicians killed this one, with the result that the next in the Harrier line was the AV-8B/GR.5 Harrier II.

Above: USMC AV-8As from VMA-513 over the Arizona desert en route to Yuma rocket range.

The Variants

Two AV-8As were modified as YAV-8B prototypes, the first of which flew in November 1978. These were followed by some four Full-Scale

Above and right: The AV-8B has a bubble canopy to improve vision, LERX, and an improved double-slotted flap wing.

SPECIFICATION

Harrier GR.5/7

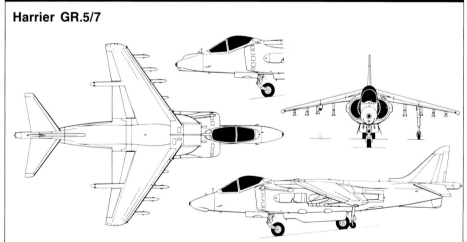

Dimensions
Length: 46ft 4in (14.12m)
Height: 11ft 7¾in (3.55m)
Wing span: 30ft 4in (9.24m)
Gross wing area: 230sq ft (21.37m²)

Weights
Empty: 12,922lb (5,861kg)
Vertical take-off: 18,950lb (8,595kg)
Maximum loaded: 31,000lb (14,061kg)

Power
1×Rolls Royce Pegasus 105 vectored thrust

turbofan rated at 21,750lb (96.67kN) static thrust
Internal fuel: 7,759lb (3,519kg)

Performance
Maximum speed: 583kt (1,075km/h)
Initial rate of climb: 50,000ft/min (254m/sec)
Service ceiling: over 50,000ft (15,250m)
Typical operational radius: 400nm (741km)
(NB: The Harrier GR.7 is essentially the GR.5 equipped for night operations).

Development (FSD) Harrier IIs, the first of which made its maiden flight at St. Louis on 15 November 1981. In appearance it differed from the previous models in many ways.

The most obvious change was the raised cockpit, which featured a bubble canopy similar to that of the Sea Harrier, but with a wrap-around one piece windshield, giving the pilot an all-round view. The other major external difference was the wing. A supercritical aerofoil, with its span increased by 5ft (1.55m) and area increased by 29sq ft (2.69m²), it also features a slightly reduced leading-edge sweep, (36deg instead of 40deg). The wing is also deeper, with an increased thickness/chord ratio, and integral tanks hold an extra 2,116lb (960kg) of fuel. The outriggers have been moved inboard, and are now housed mainly within the wing, reducing the leg fairings. The resultant narrower wheel track improves ground handling. Leading-Edge Root Extensions (LERX) form vortices over the upper surface of the wing, adding greatly to pitch response and manoeuvrability at high AoA. The ailerons are located outboard of the outriggers, while inboard are huge double-slotted flaps which, when lowered to 62deg, react with the thrust from the angled rear nozzles to give improved short take-off performance.

The engine inlets have been "tweaked" to improve internal air flow, and the capture area increased. The inlet lips have a new elliptical profile, and longer zero scarf front nozzles offer a useful thrust increment; while LIDs enhance vertical take-off and landing capabilities. They consist of two longitudinal strakes located beneath the forward fuselage, with a retractable dam at their front edge. When hovering in ground effect, the efflux bouncing back off the ground is trapped between them and effectively adds to the vertical lift component. On previous Harriers, the gun pods to a degree acted as strakes, but the hot gases could flow forward and be reingested by the engine. The dam prevents this recirculation and, as a side effect, significantly reduces engine temperatures. When making a vertical landing, earlier Harriers tended to wobble around a bit, the so-called "cobblestone effect", and then be sucked down as they settled. The Harrier II with its LIDs is far more stable, perching on its column of exhaust gas, and needing power to be reduced before it can touch down.

The structure of the Harrier II makes use of a high proportion of composite materials, approximately 26 per cent. The front fuselage, the wing structure, and the horizontal stabilizers are all made from this material, which results in a significant weight saving.

As noted earlier, the Harrier was a bit twitchy in certain low speed ranges during transition from hovering to forward flight. The GR.5/AV-8B has a new high-authority attitude hold system with pitch/roll autostabilization, which greatly improves safety margins

Above and below: Two views of the GR.5, one of the most modern versions of the Harrier.

Below: The supercritical wing and other refinements doubled the payload/range of the AV-8B.

Above: The AV-8B FSD2, with its distinctive red-and-white finish, attaches itself to a trailing hose extended from a KC-130 refuelling tanker of VMGR-352 during early trials.

The Variants

throughout the flight regime, thus reducing the pilot's workload. This has also cured the tendency of the nose to wander about in vertical flight. The flight control system is digital fly-by-wire (FBW), and the Harrier II is the first operational aircraft to make use of fibre optics, carrying light impulses instead of electrical impulses.

The cockpit layout is totally new. A large HUD with dual combiner glass, its control panel immediately below, is fitted, and multi-function displays dominate the dashboard. The GR.5 retains the moving map display of the earlier model, and it is expected that the AV-8B will have a similar system retrofitted in the near future. Controls are HOTAS, with everything the pilot needs in combat under his hands. The heart of the attack suite is the Angle Rate Bombing System (ARBS), which has enabled pilots to achieve remarkable scores on the range. ARBS consists of a laser spot tracker and a TV contrast imager working together, which can be locked onto a target. Several different attack modes can be selected, depending on the target and

the extra cockpit, and the fin is 17in (43cm) taller. The RAF planned to convert some T.4s to T.6 standard, but this was not a viable proposition. In March 1990, however, they ordered 14 two-seaters under the designation of T.10.

War does not end at sunset, and the need to operate during the hours of darkness has led to the next stage in

Above: The Harrier GR.7 has two extra hardpoints, an IR sensor and a night-vision cockpit.

the Harrier's evolution. This is the Night Attack Harrier II, which first flew in 1987. This has a fixed Forward-Looking Infra-Red (FLIR) seeker in the nose which projects a video-type image of the terrain ahead onto the

Above: The first T4 with RWR and LR/MTS just fitted.

the weapon used, for a first-pass attack.

Like earlier models, the Harrier II has a two-seat conversion trainer variant; in USMC service this is the TAV-8B. This model has a lengthened forward fuselage to accommodate

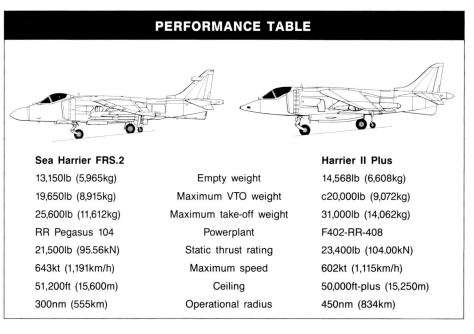

PERFORMANCE TABLE

Sea Harrier FRS.2		Harrier II Plus
13,150lb (5,965kg)	Empty weight	14,568lb (6,608kg)
19,650lb (8,915kg)	Maximum VTO weight	c20,000lb (9,072kg)
25,600lb (11,612kg)	Maximum take-off weight	31,000lb (14,062kg)
RR Pegasus 104	Powerplant	F402-RR-408
21,500lb (95.56kN)	Static thrust rating	23,400lb (104.00kN)
643kt (1,191km/h)	Maximum speed	602kt (1,115km/h)
51,200ft (15,600m)	Ceiling	50,000ft-plus (15,250m)
300nm (555km)	Operational radius	450nm (834km)

HUD, while the pilot wears Night Vision Goggles (NVGs). The cockpit lighting has been changed from white to blue/green to give compatibility with the NVGs. The third component in the night attack system is a colour digital moving map, which also displays navigation data and threat intelligence. Naturally the system is inadequate for really poor weather conditions, but it does extend the operating spectrum around-the-clock under most conditions. RAF Harrier GR.5s are to be retrofitted with the night attack system, and will subsequently become Harrier GR.7s.

While the Harrier II can carry Sidewinder AAMs for self-defence, it lacks a really effective air-to-air combat capability. The obvious next step is the Harrier II Plus: a multi-mission aircraft, proposals for which were first announced in 1987. This will be powered by the Pegasus 11-61, which gives 24,500lb st (109kN) of thrust, and which will have double the time between overhauls of previous versions. The major difference will be an advanced multi-mode radar, namely

Above: A Night Attack Harrier II of VX-5 with FLIR in the nose and two AGM-65E Mavericks.

the Hughes APG-65 as used in the McDonnell Douglas F/A-18 Hornet, which is optimized for the dual fighter/attack mission. The Harrier II Plus will be able to fly any mission currently undertaken by the AV-8B/

GR.5, and then some. Air-to-air weaponry will consist of up to six AMRAAMs, or an AMRAAM/ Sidewinder mix.

The future development of the Harrier remains uncertain, mainly due to the belief that air forces can manage by operating conventional aircraft from damaged runways. And it cannot be denied that supersonic speed is essential for the interceptor role. Supersonic variants of the Harrier using plenum chamber burning have been considered, and in fact, the P.1154, which was mooted at the outset, then cancelled in 1965, was to have been a STOVL aircraft with all-round capabilities to rival the F-4 Phantom II. Ironically, the current trend is to take a conventional fighter and enhance its STOL and manoeuvring capabilities via thrust vectoring, to provide a sort of halfway house. What they can never do with this approach is to provide a combat aircraft with a true mobile, off-site basing capability, nor one that can operate from small ships. While these two requirements are still needed — which should be as long as the requirement for effective air power exists — the future of the Harrier ought to be assured.

Above: The two-seater TAV-8B (T.10 in the RAF) is the combat capable conversion trainer.

Above: The green glow of NVGs enable the pilot to see at night but limit peripheral vision.

THE Harrier was developed as a Close Air Support/Battlefield Air Interdiction (CAS/BAI) machine, and has been cleared to carry a wide range of British, American and NATO tactical air-to-ground weapons, plus Anti-Shipping Missiles (ASM) and AAMs. The possible combinations of which are almost endless.

Harriers up to the GR.3/AV-8A have five hardpoints; two under each wing and one on the centreline. In addition, there are two belly (sometimes erroneously called shoulder) positions for gun pods. The two inboard wing pylons are plumbed for drop tanks, and typically, either 100 Imp gal (455 litre) or 300 US gal (1,135.5 litre) tanks are carried. The external load to which the GR.3/ AV-8A is cleared is 8,000lb (3,632kg), but the normal operational load rarely exceeds 5,300lb (2,406kg).

FIREPOWER

The detachable gun pods each contain a 30mm (1.18in) Aden Mk 4 with 100 rounds, although by using the feed chutes, 130 rounds can be carried to give a firing time of about 6½ sec. The rate-of-fire of the Aden is about 1,200 rounds/min., the projectile weight around eight ounces (226g), while the muzzle velocity is 2,500ft/sec (762.5m/sec). The muzzles feature a frangible protective cover which is blown away by the first shell. The shape and position of the gun pods actually allows them to act as LIDs, and when they are not carried, longitudinal strakes must be fitted in their place. It was always intended that the AV-8A would carry an American 20mm (0.8in) gun pod, but the reliability and general excellence of the 30mm (1.18in) Aden so commended itself that it

Above: Armourers load the Aden's 30mm ammunition before a GR.3's practice mission.

was retained in USMC service.

For air-to-ground work, a variety of ordnance is carried. The two inboard pylons can each accommodate two 1,000lb (454kg) bombs. These can be free-fall, retarded Snakeyes, or laser-guided Paveways, with a fifth weapon on the centreline hardpoint. BL755, Rockeye or Matra Cluster Bomb Units (CBUs) can be carried in all five positions. For many years, the preferred RAF weapon for the CAS mission was the 68mm (2.68in) SNEB rocket, 18 of which could be carried in each of five Matra 155 launch pods, but CBUs are now the preferred scatter weapon, with retarded or "smart" bombs for specific tasks. In USMC service, the AV-8A has been cleared to launch the monster 5in (12.7cm) Zuni unguided

rocket. In the anti-shipping role, two Martel or Harpoon medium-range guided missiles can be carried on the inboard pylons, although in practice they rarely are.

For self-defence, the AIM-9B Sidewinder AAM was cleared for Harrier use as far back as 1968, with one carried on each outboard wing pylon. While the USMC have routinely carried this AAM from the outset, the RAF failed to follow through with this weapon. The mad scramble to get the Task Force to the South Atlantic in 1982 saw the immediate release of a picture of a No 1(F) Squadron Harrier GR.3 at RAF Wittering carrying

Below: The underneath of the AV-8B reveals its ordnance carrying hardpoint potential.

a pair of these AAMs. What was not revealed at the time was the fact that it had no wiring, although this was quickly added.

The Sea Harrier FRS.1 was always intended to carry the AIM-9 Sidewinder and was so equipped from the outset. Combat experience in 1982 showed that two AAMs were inadequate and lacked combat persistence, and double-launchers were cleared for use soon after. The same conflict also highlighted the shortcomings of the Sidewinder, even though the latest AIM-9L variant was used. While theoretically the Lima is an all-angle weapon, in 1982 it was invariably launched from the target's rear quadrant. While the static range of the Lima is 11nm (20km), this is vastly reduced down at sea level where most combat took place, and shrinks

Right: A Harrier II releasing a pair of Snakeye retarded bombs during separation trials.

Below: A selection of stores carried by the FRS.1. The inboard wing stations have a capacity of 2,000lb (907kg), twice that of those outboard.

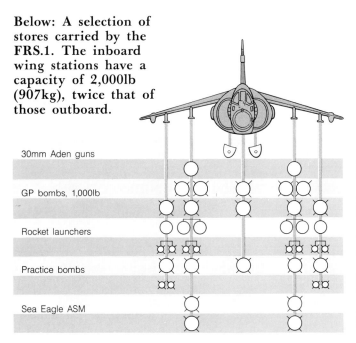

30mm Aden guns

GP bombs, 1,000lb

Rocket launchers

Practice bombs

Sea Eagle ASM

Below: A selection of the AV-8B's stores which are fixed on six wing and three fuselage stations with a maximum load of 9,200lb (4,173kg).

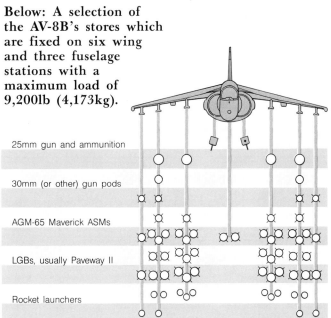

25mm gun and ammunition

30mm (or other) gun pods

AGM-65 Maverick ASMs

LGBs, usually Paveway II

Rocket launchers

The Weapons and Missions

Harriers operated by the Indian Navy.

The Sea Harrier carries much the same air-to-surface ordnance as its RAF counterpart. One difference is the Royal Navy standard rocket pod, which houses 36 2in (50mm) projectiles. To reduce logistics problems in the South Atlantic, the GR-3 was quickly cleared to carry this weapon, rather than the SNEB pod. Naturally there is a greater anti-shipping emphasis with a naval aircraft, and the Sea Harrier can carry two BAe Sea Eagles, a medium-range, sea skimming ASM developed from the Martel.

IMPROVING THE PAYLOAD

The improved performance of the AV-8B/GR.5 allows a considerable improvement in the Harrier's payload/range. This is reflected in the fact that the Harrier II has no less than nine hardpoints in addition to the two cannon stations. While the maximum ordnance load of 9,200lb (4,173kg) is not a great advance over the previous bird, it can haul it a great deal farther. The Harrier II can carry a load of 16 500lb (227kg) Mk 82 bombs out to a radius of 150nm (278km) using 7,500lb (3,402kg) of fuel; or six Mk 82s out to 450nm (834km) with 11,500 lb (5,216kg) of fuel. A further

dynamically even more when the target is retreating at high speed. The result was that in several cases, although the missiles were launched from quite close static ranges, they fell short. The combat record of the AIM-9L in the South Atlantic was good, but not good enough. What was needed was a missile with a longer reach, coupled with beyond visual range capability, while retaining the launch-and-leave facility of the Sidewinder. The ability to operate effectively in cloud or mist, where the Infra-Red (IR) seeker of the Sidewinder does not perform well, was

Above: A bewildering array of ordnance arranged in front of the AV-8B. To this should now be added Maverick, Hellfire, Harpoon and AMRAAM missiles.

another essential. These requirements are being met for the Sea Harrier FRS.2 by the AIM-120 AMRAAM, a medium-range missile which can be launched from a distance at a predicted position, and which uses active radar terminal homing. The other AAM used is the French-designed Matra R550 Magic, an IR homer like the AIM-9, which is carried by Sea

Above: A USMC AV-8B with two Maverick air-to-ground missiles, the scourge of Iraq.

Right: The carriage of 300 US gal long range tanks has greatly enhanced combat ranges.

advantage is that whatever the load, the take-off run is greatly reduced. Two hardpoints are dedicated to Sidewinders, and are located at the front of the outriggers, where double-launchers can be carried. Four of the wing points are plumbed, and are cleared to carry 300 US gal (1,135.5 litre) drop tanks, as well as the smaller standard tanks. The ordnance carried is very much the same as that of

Above: The Hellfire anti-tank missile proved its potency against Iraq's armour in Kuwait.

previous versions, although the ARBS has greatly improved accuracy of delivery. The RAF retain SNEB pods for their inshore anti-shipping role, while the USMC have a recently obtained clearance for the AGM-65 Laser Maverick air-to-ground missile (AGM). This last weapon should give much greater lethality; previous variants of this missile worked on optical or Imaging Infra-Red (IIR) contrast, and problems with breaking lock could occur.

The GR.5 and AV-8B no longer carry the 30mm (1.18in) Aden cannon. The new weapons have a 25mm calibre, with a smaller and lighter projectile. This, however, is more than compensated for by higher rates-of-

Centre, right: This Indian Navy Harrier is armed with R.550 Magic, a French homing missile.

Above: The Sea Harrier is cleared to carry two large Sea Eagle anti-shipping missiles.

The Weapons and Missions

Left: GR.5 with a full load of seven BL755 cluster bombs and two Sidewinders.

Below, left: A Sea Harrier FRS.2 with four AIM-120 AMRAAM missiles and two drop tanks.

fire, improved ballistic qualities, and greater muzzle velocity which, range for range, gives the shells much higher kinetic energy. The Harrier GR.5 carries two 25mm (1in) Aden pods, each with 100 rounds of ammunition. The Aden 25 is a gas-operated revolver cannon with a rate-of-fire between 1,650 and 1,850 rounds/min, and a muzzle velocity of 3,445ft (1,051m)/sec. By contrast, the AV-8B carries a totally new Gatling-type weapon, the GAU-12/U. Powered by a pneumatic drive motor, the GAU-12/U has five rotating barrels carried in the left-hand pod, while the right-hand pod holds 300 rounds of ammunition, with a linkless feed connecting the two. Like all Gatling types, the rate-of-fire is

high at 3,600 rounds/min, and the muzzle velocity is 3,500ft (1,067m)/sec.

Weaponry for the GR.7/Night Attack Harrier remains the same as that for the GR.5/AV-8B. The Harrier II Plus will carry the AIM-120 AMRAAM as described for the Sea Harrier FRS.2, as its primary air-to-air weapon, in addition to the many air-to-surface weapons already cleared for use.

FLEXIBLE BASING

The primary Harrier mission has always been CAS/BAI, with a secondary reconnaissance capability. Only latterly has air defence been added to the list. Its operational usage revolves

about its unique STOVL capability, which enables it to operate without benefit of long concrete runways, or vast and costly aircraft carriers.

Both airfields and conventional aircraft carriers are enormously high-value targets, which a potential enemy would consider worth the expenditure of a great deal of effort to take out. The STOVL capability of the Harrier allows it to operate from small, temporary dispersed bases, which are both difficult to locate and easy to move; or from small and relatively low-value ships. The difficulty of grounding, let alone destroying, a deployed Harrier unit, is therefore many times more difficult compared to a conventional tactical fighter squadron. In addition, dispersed basing allows the Harrier to be deployed far closer to the main battle area than would otherwise be practical, thereby giving the tremendous advantage of quick reaction.

It is blindingly obvious that speed of reaction is essential for the CAS/BAI mission. An infantry or armoured unit in trouble wants assistance NOW, not in an hour's time. The closer to the forward line of troops the aircraft is based, the quicker it can bring air power to bear. A fuelled and armed Harrier at readiness 50nm (93km) back from the front can be lining up its attack run in less than ten minutes.

All attack missions are planned by balancing fuel needs against weapon loads; the less fuel needed, the greater the load of ordnance that can be carried. This is the distance/payload equation, where distance also equals time-in-transit. Many conventional

Above: An intermediate type, the GR.5A, under a camouflaged net during an exercise in Europe.

Right, below: Inflatable shelters allow ground crews to maintain air worthiness in the field.

attack aircraft can carry greater loads over longer distances, but based well back from the fighting, they not only cannot reach the scene for the initial attack so quickly, but they cannot return so often during the course of the day — and probably not at all if their airfield has been bombed while they were away. In addition, their longer transit time gives an adversary more chance of intercepting them en route. The ability of the Harrier to return to the attack again and again within a very short space of time, enables it to deliver a greater weight of ordnance within a given space of time than many theoretically more capable fighters.

In peacetime exercises, Harriers have often flown as many as ten sorties a day for up to three days, although this rate of flying cannot be maintained over extended periods. Its reaction time is short, to the benefit of the beleaguered friendly ground troops and the disadvantage of enemy interceptors, while its runway cannot be knocked out. Only a handful of

Harriers operate from each dispersal site, and if by chance a base is discovered and attacked, losses will thus be minimal. Machines airborne at the time will simply divert to another dispersal site. In all, the effort needed to knock out an entire dispersed Harrier squadron would be quite disproportionate to the effort, and probable losses to the local air defences, that would be incurred by an attacking force.

Harriers are normally based on a conventional airfield, because it is more efficient for maintenance, training and logistics, and they only disperse into the surrounding countryside when hostilities threaten. Should a Pearl Harbor-type attack catch them there, and the field be rendered totally unusable by Conventional Take-Off and Landing (CTOL) aircraft, Harriers will still be able to operate by hover-taxying at a light weight to a suitable, i.e. less pockmarked, spot where they can be fuelled and armed before heading off to their

dispersed "hides". In short, the Harrier is the nearest thing to a guarantee of continued air power.

For peacetime exercises, dispersed bases are usually in or near woodland, which offers good cover from prying eyes and cameras. Take-off and landing is done on metal plank pads, which shield against ground erosion. The Harrier has demonstrated over and over that it can operate quite happily from quite small woodland clearings. In fact, during the sales drive in the 1970s, a short golf course was laid out on BAe's airfield at Dunsfold, and visitors were invited to have a game. This was soon to be rudely interrupted by a Harrier landing on the third green in among the trees. Apparently everyone was most impressed — except for the Japanese, who take their golf much too seriously!

In wartime, urban basing would be preferred. IR devices have made woodland basing vulnerable to detection, and current thinking is to base Harrier detachments in built-up areas.

The Weapons and Missions

Above: An Arctic take-off using this quickly made runway proves the flexibility of the Harrier.

Here they would be housed in buildings, factories, warehouses; even supermarkets with the fronts knocked out to permit access would do, the only other requirement being access to a hardstanding suitable for take-off and landing, such as a car park. While under cover, the Harriers would be nearly impossible to detect, and the proximity of a road network would ease maintenance and logistical problems.

Logistics has always been the main problem of dispersed basing. While proximity to the battle area reduces the amount of fuel needed, the short reaction time and potentially high number of sorties would increase the amount of munitions needed on site. Often woodland sites do not have good road links, and the number of helicopters available for resupply is limited. Urban basing would ease the problems of resupply considerably, in addition to being difficult to detect.

The benefits of the ski jump for take-off/payload performance are well known. It has been unofficially suggested that dispersed sites could be selected near roads on the brow of a hill, thus providing a suitable ramp effect. If a few farm buildings were at hand, with a suitably sized barn, that would be just perfect. Another option

would be to form ramps against the sides of Hardened Aircraft Shelters (HAS) that proliferate on most NATO airfields. Something like three dozen ramps could be provided, with adequate run-up space, for much less than the cost of a single orthodox runway. The accepted wisdom is that a conventional airfield is vulnerable to attack, and its runway is the most vulnerable area. This poses the question, how much less vulnerable (barring nuclear attack) is an airfield if it is not runway-dependent? Knocking out three dozen ski-jumps would be immeasurably harder for an attacking force than a single runway. As a by-product, the ramps would provide extra protection for the hardened shelters!

AT SEA

The requirements of the USMC are rather different than those of the RAF. Their primary requirement is to provide air cover and support for their amphibious landing forces. While this could be done by the giant US Navy aircraft carriers and their assigned Air Wings, this would have certain short-

Above: An AV-8B makes its deck landing, one of the most testing times for any pilot.

comings. The first handicap is that of cost. Huge nuclear-powered carriers do not come cheap, and the supporting group of Aegis missile cruisers and other vessels are even more expensive. It would be unwise to risk such a high value target too close to a well-guarded coastline, and it must therefore stand well out to sea, not least to give itself

Below: FRS.1 flying above HMS *Hermes* shortly before the war in the South Atlantic.

Above: AV-8As of VMA-231 in a Norwegian fjord. From here they could offer close air support.

sea room for flying off heavily-laden jets, and recovering them afterwards. The penalty to be paid for this solution is in reaction time, which is always at a premium. Furthermore, something like half the aircraft complement of a nuclear-powered aircraft carrier is engaged in defensive or force multiplication tasks, leaving perhaps 20 or so aircraft out of an Air Wing with approximately 85 aircraft, to support the landing force. The USMC need air cover; they need CAS and they need it quickly. They also need to establish shore bases at the earliest possible moment, to give organic air cover. With conventional fast jets, this is very difficult, if not impossible,

and USMC AV-8 squadrons routinely fly from commando and helicopter carriers. To operate the AV-8 there is no need to steam into the wind prior to launch, or to assist recovery. The ship can even be at anchor, close in behind the landing force, while metal plank landing pads can be set up ashore within a few hours of a suitable site being secured. Flexible fuel bladders, munitions and other stores, plus groundcrew, are then flown in by helicopter. The AV-8s then fly a mission from the ship, using the forward location for refuelling and rearming when needed.

While USMC AV-8s rely to a degree on fighter cover being provided by CTOL carrier aircraft, it was recognized at an early stage that some form of self-defence capability was needed. This took the form of Side-

winder AAMs, but carriage of these weapons sterilized a couple of pylons, reducing the air-to-surface ordnance load. This problem has been solved on the Harrier II, which has a dedicated Sidewinder hardpoint forward of each outrigger housing, leaving the main pylons free for air-to-surface ordnance.

The need to intercept Soviet Tupolev Tu-95 Bears in mid-Atlantic led to the Sea Harrier FRS.1; the first of the breed to carry radar. While it lacks supersonic speed for this role, it has a relatively long loiter time, and is able to operate in weather conditions that would ground CTOL carrier fighters. While no doubt the admirals would have preferred a fleet carrier equipped with F-14 Tomcats, the Sea Harriers offer at least some air-defence capability.

There is an old saying: "You never

The Weapons and Missions

Left: En route to the Falklands a Sea Harrier lines up to port to select its spot for landing.

fight the war for which you are equipped and trained; you fight the war you have got with what is to hand.'' Twice so far in the Harrier's service life this has been proven. The first time was in the mid-1970s, when Guatemala began to threaten Belize (formerly British Honduras), and six Harriers from No. 1 (F) Sqn, RAF, were detached there (Belize International Airport has the only hard runway in the country, which a single strike could render unusable by CTOL fighters). The unit remains in Belize as No. 1417 Flight, RAF. The second instance was the Falklands War in 1982.

THE FALKLANDS WAR

Operation ''*Corporate*'' was mounted in April of that year to recover the Falkland Islands from Argentine occupation. It was totally unlike any other military operation in history, in that it was conducted more than 4,000 miles (6,436km) from the nearest friendly base; Ascension Island, in the South Atlantic. Normally no nation could have attempted it without the assistance of a Fleet aircraft carrier, but Sea Harriers (later augmented by

Above: With one Sea Harrier on deck alert protectively shrouded GR.3s line the *Atlantic Conveyor*.

RAF GR.3s), flying from the decks of HMS *Hermes* and HMS *Invincible*, provided organic air power.

The small Harrier force was going up against a numerically superior and well-equipped opponent. It was generally considered that a subsonic fighter would be outclassed by a supersonic one, and the Dassault Mirages and Israeli Aircraft Industries (IAI) Daggers of the Argentine Air Force had previously built an enviable reputation in Israeli service. In addition, the Argentine Air Force and Navy flew the McDonnell Douglas A-4 Skyhawk, a nimble attack aircraft which could theoretically outmanoeuvre the Sea Harrier in close combat.

At this juncture it should be stated that the Harrier is not the most agile performer in the close combat arena as its wing loading is slightly on the high side, a factor that was later to lead to the big wing Harrier II. Viffing (swivelling the nozzles in forward flight) is popularly supposed to give the Harrier an unsurpassed turn performance, but in fact it only enables an extra half g loading to be attained, which is not a lot, at the expense of a considerable speed loss. While it certainly does permit some extremely unorthodox manoeuvres to be carried out, it was never to be used in the South Atlantic, simply because the need never arose. It may, however, prove to be invaluable in the future.

Pending the arrival of the RAF GR.3s, the Sea Harriers had to perform the tasks of both air-defence and attack. In the former role they were handicapped. The lack of Airborne Early Warning (AEW) meant that the wasteful system of standing Combat Air Patrols (CAP) had to be used. This was aggravated by the fact

the carriers, the final quartet flew down to the Task Force, another 4,000 miles. The whole operation was an exercise in sheer flexibility impossible for any other fighter.

Ten Harriers were lost during the conflict, five in operational accidents, and five to enemy ground fire. Over 2,000 sorties were flown, and aircraft availability was never less than 95 per cent at the start of each day. It is true to say that the recovery of the Falkland Islands could never have been attempted had it not been for the Harrier and Sea Harrier. It should also be considered that the Argentinian-held airfield at Stanley had a hard runway some 4,000ft (1,220m) long, which was too short to be safely used by their fast jets. If they too had had Harriers . . .!

Below: AV-8B over desert sands. Losses in the Gulf were minimal and damage inflicted devastating.

WAR IN THE GULF

The AV-8Bs of the USMC saw intensive action in the Kuwait theatre of operations in the early months of 1991. Marine squadrons VMA-311, 331 and 542, each with 12 aircraft, were based in Dhahran, while a small AV-8B detachment from VMA-223 operated from the assault ship USS *Saipan*. They took part in the initial softening up of Iraqi positions, and were active in providing close air support during the Iraqi army's raid on Khafra towards the end of January. With the opening of the land offensive on 22 February of that year, they reverted to their primary roles of battlefield air interdiction and giving close air support to Marine and allied ground forces. Losses of AV-8Bs totalled four, three to ground fire and one to a non-combat cause. The AV-8B performed well during its baptism of fire.

Above: GR.3s of No 1417 Flight maintain a presence in Belize (formerly British Honduras).

that the two Royal Navy carriers had to be based well to the East, resulting in a long transit time and a correspondingly reduced time-on-station. Furthermore, the radar had no real look-down capability, which often allowed the ultra low-level Argentine attackers to escape. Despite everything, the Sea Harriers succeeded in shooting down a total of 22 enemy aircraft in air combat without loss.

The Harrier GR.3s of No. 1 (F) Sqn, RAF, set off in a southerly direction on 3 May, flying non-stop from RAF St. Mawgan in Cornwall to Ascension Island, 4,000 miles (6,436km) away. With their bolt-on probes fitted, they refuelled in flight five times *en route* in what was a nine-hour ferry mission. While most completed the journey aboard container ships before hover-taxying across to

FOR an aircraft with so much operational flexibility and potential, the Harrier has made singularly little impact on the world market over the past twenty years; and had it not received such an enthusiastic reception from the USMC, this would have been even less. Much of this has to do with fashion: the requirement, real or imagined, for supersonic speed and preferably Mach 2; what American defence analyst Pierre Sprey has referred to as "Mach 2 Madness". Had the P.1154 gone ahead when first projected, all Harriers would have been supersonic multi-role fighters, and the story might have been very different. As it stands, all who have seen the Harrier demonstrated have professed to be very impressed, but few have bought it.

The first operational user was the RAF, with No. 1 (F) Squadron based at RAF Wittering; Nos. 3 and 4 (F) Squadrons based in Germany; and No. 233 Operational Conversion Unit (OCU), which is also at RAF Wittering. Of these, No. 1 Sqn has had the most eventful time. It was they who provided a detached Flight for Belize, and it was they who flew south to the Falkland Islands in 1982, in the course of which conflict they gained the title "battle proven" for the Harrier. Assigned to NATO, in the event of a war in Europe they would deploy to northern Norway where, resplendent in winter camouflage, they exercise on a regular basis. They have also exercised in many other countries, in one of which they acquired what must be the most original paint job ever worn by the type. Some time in the mid-1970s a detachment visited Dijon in France to fly with the "Cicognes". During this visit, they "zapped" one of the French Mirages, painting a Harrier doing something rather rude to the host unit's stork emblem. Naturally the French retaliated. On the last night of the visit, they set out to paint the two-seat Harrier, traditionally flown by the detachment commander, a bright gloss pink. Apparently they ran out of red at an early stage, but the result was still spectacular. Harrier variants flown by the RAF have been GR.1, GR.1A, T.2,

Below: Sea Harrier Mk 51 of the Indian Navy's White Lions Squadron prior to delivery.

Below: A factory fresh EAV-8B of the Spanish Navy flying near vertically in its check flight.

and T.2A. Currently in service are the GR.3, T.4, and GR.5. Still to come are the GR.7 and T.10.

Numerically, the largest operator of the type is the USMC, who operate the AV-8A and TAV-8A, although these early models are being withdrawn to storage as they are replaced by the AV-8B and TAV-8B, and the AV-8C; a designation given to 47 AV-8As which were upgraded with LIDs, OBOGS, and other mainly avionics improvements. These models are being followed by the Night Attack Harrier II and, at a future date, the Harrier II Plus air-defence fighter variant.

The Sea Harriers flown by the Fleet Air Arm (FAA) of the Royal Navy have seen the most action. The FAA operates two front-line Sea Harrier FRS.1 squadrons, Nos. 800 and 801; and a headquarters and training squadron, No. 899, based at Royal Naval Air Station (RNAS) Yeovilton, Somerset. A combination of upgraded and new-build aircraft will see these

Above: The Italian Navy carrier *Guiseppe Garibaldi* will carry Harrier II Plus fighters aboard.

Above: Under the designation AV-8S Matador the Spanish Navy has had AV-8As for years.

units equipped with the Sea Harrier FRS.2 by the end of 1992. For pilot conversion work the FAA uses two-seater Sea Harrier T.4NS.

The Sea Harrier, in its Mk. 51 guise, is also used by the Indian Navy, operating from the aircraft carrier *Vikrant*; and T.60 trainers are used for conversion work. Another carrier is

planned, and it seems likely that a further batch of Harriers will be acquired by India at some future date, possibly the Harrier II Plus.

The Spanish Navy now operates a

complement of five AV-8S Matadors from the aircraft carrier *Dedalo*, and eight EAV-8Bs from the new *Principe de Asturias*. Plans are in hand to replace the latter aircraft with a squadron of Harrier II Plus within the next three years, and it is not impossible that a second new carrier will be built in due course, which will require the purchase of even more aircraft.

The most recent member of the Harrier club is Italy, which is expected to order 15 Harrier II Plus and two TAV-8Bs for its new aircraft carrier *Guiseppe Garibaldi*. It is also reported that the keel of a second carrier has been laid down, which will increase the Italian Harrier requirement even more substantially.

INDEX